Peasant Poetry (Verse)

Margin notes to a life

Simple, Silly and Serious

Published 2023 by Don Hayward,
8 Huron Lane, Goderich, Ontario, Canada N7A 3Y2
ISBN: 978-1-7380641-0-6

2023, Don Hayward
All rights reserved.

No one may reproduced, store in a retrieval system, or transmitted in any form or by any means, electronic, mechanical, recording or otherwise, any part of this publication without the prior written permission of Don Hayward.

Front cover: Don Hayward 1969
Back cover: Don takes a shot, on the High Falls ice rink 1955

All bad poetry springs from genuine feeling. – Oscar Wilde

I am still the little boy wanting one person, maybe me, to understand my soul and hug.

"The memories, even the hard ones now sweetened by time, roiled in his mind as the water did at the bottom of the falls, with big splashes of time suddenly leaping into view. When they washed against the hard surface of reality, they left a bright sheen, a memory of their passing."
–From Echo of the Whip-poor-will (Don Hayward – 2018)

I do not intend the verses below to aspire to, or imitate great or even good poetry. If the reader approaches verse from a literary perspective, I suggest they not bother proceeding further. As the sub-title says, these are the margin notes to my life. I have recorded my thoughts and feelings at various times and from an early age have expressed them in crude verse and rhyme. The quality will be uneven. I have included things here that evoke something in me. Re-reading these makes me re-examine my thoughts, feelings and attitudes and give me a sense of change, if not progress. There is no definite chronology here. The verses are not in rigid order from youth to now.

Some of the thoughts, attitudes and feelings may not apply now to my thinking. Notes, after all, exist as mere reminders of a special place in a story. We grow and learn as a story develops. In the same way, the male-centric nature of some of this reflects both the times when entitled males were generally ignorant of gender bias and the reality that I intend the male in much of this to be the writer.

My reactions to reading these records will likely escape the reader. Those might become the subject of another verse or two some night when I immerse myself in these and feel melancholy. For now, they remind me of people, places and circumstance that are important.

I hope that you find these interesting and perhaps, if good at all, they will raise a smile, a thought or a tear.

I write no deeper poem
But thought and rhyme
My life's trail to mark
With blazing on the bark
That I might then divine
My shadowed way to home

Within this memory

Aspen birch and pine
Blazing October
Colours this heart of mine
Setting feet restless
Upon memory's road
Visiting places that
Be no more
But living wild
Within this memory

Words

Words that brush the mind
Birthing images
Thoughts and feelings
Desire for the view
But at the end
May they ignite
Love and caring
Embracing all the new
I look at the cosmic wonder
In its faithful eternity
And give thanks
At my brief privilege of being.

Simple

*The only remembered snippet of my first ever poem, Grade 5.
Perhaps not a poem worth remembering, but it was my first.*

Nature's little parachutes
Falling to the ground
Nature's little parachutes
Making ne're a sound.

***

I awoke one day
In simpler times
The clang and clash long gone
My thoughts were of food
And fire and love
My heart was full of song.

***

Gone are the children
Simple pleasures and fun
Carried into adulthood
On times constant run

***

Memories softly drop
Upon your ken
Rolling up the years
From now, to then.

Letter to a friend December 19/68

Now permit me
To take you
Upon my knee
As we sit
Here by the fire

Ever mind the
North-east wind
That plucks
The hydro wires
(Mournfully, of course)
Piling snow in ridges

Listen
As I tell
Tales of man
Woe and victory
Laughter and tears
Dreams and terrors
Woven into
Broadcloth
Many hued
Of infinite
Warp and woof

Change knees
Bank the fire
Breath… slowly
Now…

And thus

The tale ends
You climb down
From upon my knee
I move
To hold you near

You fade
Into the fire
The flames embrace
As you smile
Soothing
Fading away
Fading… faint

I sigh
In thanks
Aware
Of warm comfort
You have given

Picture and poetry

One grabs the scene
To freeze it still
In perfect line as it had been
Settled there unchanging will
And forever what we see
A place that no longer be
A rhyme explores the essence true
The instant that would then renew
Its perfect hint of what will be
That finds the soul of what we see
And tells its tale to you and me

Oh, dear child,

Wonder what the world might be
Wonder at the growing tree
Wonder at the sky so blue
And on waking
Wonder at the dew.

Life

Candle flame
Pure and clean
But then
Again
You flicker

Origins

Earth cries tears of joy
That the sea embraces
Then flings them
Upon the shore
Where myriad life
In the quiet pools of warmth
Frolic in our happiness.

Naming

Why must we find a name
For every big and little thing?
Where is the profit to know
The name of a thing
As if we own it
Or possess some eternal cleverness?
Do not the nameless stars shine
Shine on, even unseen and un-named?
Is not the full moon worthy of our awe
Without being Hunters' or Harvest or Winter?
Perhaps we circumscribe the world
To own it
But then, we circumscribe ourselves
Owned and shackled
All the while not knowing
We are part of it all
Unnamed by the universe
And free.

Happiness of friends

We can scrabble and fight
Over grander things
Striving to see who wins
But creaking gate
Welcoming friends
Happiness always brings

We will be free.

Do not mind
My rude hovel
Its handmade door
Welcoming you
To my rough dirt floor
Onions hanging from the joists
Tack and tools
Pegged to walls
Wooden shutter protecting
A glassless window
Cast iron kettle
Bubbling on the hearth
Tin plate of stew
Hot
Waiting for you
When we sit in friendship
And take that cup of tea
Then even though we have not things
My friend, we will be free.

Love

Love is a deepening sea
Lashed by storms and tide
Smashed upon rocky shore
Dark forests by its side
It flows forever with us
Gentle currents that carry us on
Beneath the stars and moonscapes
Into the brightening dawn.

Velvet night

Oh to bed upon soft straw
And the sweetly scented bough
Neath the starry velvet night
With sighs and dreams and thou

The humbling flow

When my mind embraces turmoil
My heart a beating race
I sit beneath the stars
Beneath their placid pace
Knowing that unchanging
In human time they go
My soul absorbs the timeless
The constant, humbling flow.

Sinusoid of Hope

The human heart flies ever on
The constant sinusoid between
Hope and raw despair
Travelling ever higher
On a promise oh so rare
To reach bright stars and linger
Briefly balanced there
Then plunge in sweep and cry
On the deep and darkened slope
But then in constant struggle
Rise ever higher on the hope
To soar and laugh in careless glee
As the darkened depths we flee

Into the sweet the warming sun
To loiter where we had begun.

Diane

And young
With hopes
And dreams
And love
Spilling out
Through life
Through years
Seeping through our hearts
Sweet, sincere warmth
Sustaining
Her five, her fourteen
And the uncounted
All from that little
Fragile heart
Smiling into our souls.

Aurora

You are the universe come calling
Dancing in the sky
Your shining shimmering dancing light
Pleasing in the eye.
Sweeping across the golden cold
Of the northern arch above
We stand in awe and reverence
To your sharing of your love.

Dad One

I remember his soft touch
His smile, his laugh, his praise and such
I do not sit and wait in gloom
His memory's always in the room.

Dad Two

There are no monuments raised in parks
But eternal memories in our hearts
Tears, love, laughter, smiles we knew
The joy we have knowing you
A heart that loved, a mind that sought
Two strong hands that good have wrought
A life of hope, one of cheer
Loved by ones you held so dear
Then in your hour of pain
Like the garden your Lord did gain
No betrayal of trust was seen
Standing firm, in faith serene
Now you have peace at last
Safely in your maker's grasp

Went to visit Mom in her last hours

When sunset comes
The shadows deepen
And we struggle
In the glooming
With only memories there
The warmth of day lingers still
The smiles, the love, the care.

Ode to Mom
High Falls memories

How many...
Walks on the Big Eddy Road
Workbooks of ours that you would hold
Showers in the pump room of old Number One
Blueberries picked in the afternoon sun
Dashes beneath the spraying log flume
Pansies and roses coaxed into bloom
Aprils with maple's wonderful smell
Stories of the town would you tell
Pies and nappies and sealing jars
August evenings the wonder of the stars
Lessons of life often told
Stories from your memory, all of gold
Baloney sandwiches at Clear Lake Beach

Sugar donuts, two for each
Fish and chips on Little Current dock
Coal boats working around the clock
Times climbing Grandma's Wellington stairs
Aunts, uncles and cousins greeting at theirs
Fishing lines wet in Number Two race
Pickerel dinners right after grace
Games of five hundred, cards and all
Saturday dances at High Falls hall.
Many memories from mind did fall
Because we though them just too small
Things now we would give instead
To have these memories again in our head.

Thank you Mother

The Mother we know
In December's snow
Is the Mother we knew in June
With the earth full of promise
The sun full upon us
Buds beginning to bloom
Her sweet eyes would twinkle
From a face with no wrinkle
Her love and her dreams were for all.
She raised us all higher
To dream and aspire
'til the time the trumpets would call.

From Old Albert

I dreamt I had a daughter
Living here with me
Sharing smiles and sorrows
Beneath the talking tree.

Wildwood

Oh to dance in the wildwood
Soft shadows and breeze caressing
Music of the songbird calling
Crickets in their time
Silent trees enfolding
In this our hour sublime
Oh the sweetness of our dancing
Frolic forgetting time
Soft smile and kiss enticing
In this our hour sublime

21-2-72

I ordered a spring
From Woollies
One size
Large
With flowers
They delivered it
On account
Of you I tried
To wrap it with
A brightening bow

But it burst
Forth and showered
Petals over all

April is a tease

April rains
Have their pains
Especially when they're icy
So blow away
You freezing day
You're making spring too pricy

April is not the cruellest month

April is not the cruellest month
It gives us back our forgotten life
Reminders of our failing weakness
Those soon to be forgiven
By restoring growing life
That bursts from mud
Brown and dirt of winter
Cold rushing water that soon
Becomes the warmth of life
It flies on wing
Scampers on delicate feet
Slides on bellies low
Feeding our hearts and bodies
So that when winter's sleep returns
We have the will and the means
To wait for April's fickle store.

Human arrogance

When the wind blows
It shakes the sea
When we blow
We cool our tea
And so we should
Unless we smash our cup
Upon the floor instead

Your Smile

When you smile
When you frown
When you rage or laugh
The way your brain
Has shaped your face
Is simply nice by half.

23-8-72

HOT AS HELL
ISN'T IT?
He who only
Was it last
January
Intoned
Between beers
The heat content
Of a witch's tit
And how the air
Was equally

Dry and cold
Now drinking
The same chilled
Beer talking
About the weather

June ain't June no more

June is boiling up all over
Baking the birds and bees and trees
We see the summer
It will be a bummer
Gotta wait for winter
Can we have a hint or
Maybe we'll just freeze
June is acting really strangely
Cooler cats are nowhere seen
Now we have the heat
You know it can't be beat
Maybe in the autumn
We will bottom
By one or two degrees.

Blustery summer day

Wind and water
Play in a plastic sky
Maelstrom of wind
Pleasing our humble eye

Summer High Falls 1964

It is the gentlest season of the year
With melancholy calls of birds you hear
The flight of bees, and the roar
Of the imitating mower
Trimming some dustless carpet
Here is the realm of hollow hours
Of dusty days, muddy moods
Calloused hands ... and soft, black with soil
And backs burnt brown in honest toil
Create the beauty, which could be ours.
The silence is tickled with the laughter
Of children, enjoying the here-after
You too are tempted to go in
Reward yourself with an oiling swim
"To keep the body working as it should."
Then... as the fly net is lifted it seems
The world awakes ... not sleeps
The clatter of frogs from below
Beyond the hill, the hoot of an owl
And a whip-poor-will
Signal the heavenly parade to begin
And with a cradling moon
Sinking in the west
One returns to home
And to rest

Autumn One

The mists of autumn
Take my heart
Over memory's dewy verge
Drawing my being nearer
Until this grey universe
With my soul shall merge.

Autumn Two

Autumn begins
With the promise of salvation
From summer's heat
Autumn ends
With the promise of mercy
From winter's wrath

December

December stalks
Slumping surly toward us
The land holds its breath
Waiting
For winter's winds of wrath
November strangely stubborn
Flaunting like September
Refusing to let its gentle grip
Release us to our fate
But to the north
The creak and crash of the frozen
Unity of land and sky
Creeps into our senses

Wintertime

Wintertime... and the living is freezy
Lakes are frozen
And the drifts are high
Well...your father's stuck
And your Momma's gone looking
Hush little Baby...
Little baby, don't you cry.

But the Land

You know not the north
Unless you have walked
The frozen windswept shores
Feeling the bite
Of sand snow
Lancing into your cheeks
Riding upon bitter
Unforgiving
Relentless, northern gales.

You know not the north
Unless you have felt
Its awesome silence
And humbling ice-cold breath.
That spares nothing
But the land.

In nature's face

The ice came
And lightly touched
The browns and greys and sleeping greens
Silvering all in the dancing light
Bows bend to touch the Earth
And so we must follow
Humble
In the face of nature's beauty and power

Sunlight

Harsh sunlight falls hard
Onto the canopy of green
But feeds and nourishes
Filtering through
Reflecting, refracting dancing
Down the leaves there found
Until
It gently kisses the warming ground

Nature sings

The wings, the wings
Carry seasons in
Riding southerly zephyrs
Stooping mice and rabbits
From piling summer drafts
To feathers furling
On northern wintery blasts
Nature sings, nature sings

Cosmic dance

Venus and moon
Dance to a tune
Played by a million stars
They court in the dawn
To dusk they belong
Occasionally touching Mars
But with the sparkling dew
Beneath brightening blue
They fade to a memory of ours.

Last light

We sat and held
The last of the light
Softly in our sight
And the memories rippled
Like the evening waters
Gently, to the far shore.

Dreams

Faint fancies of the night
Drifting on idle wings
Half-remembered heartaches
Childhood follies
A thousand wanderings
Real and remote
As midnight stars
Brilliant as the sun

Black as the demon soul
Viewed through sleep-fogged eyes
And in she shimmering
Sunbaked noon
The desert-pool that is
But is not
And never shall be
And always passing... passing
Gone

2-4-71

I hate the night
Stalking softly
Over the world
Hiding the secret
Dangers and horrors
That shoot swiftly
From behind
Spit from
The mouths of hell

I hate the night
Coming quickly
Down the hills
Shattering the warm
Lazy July evenings
That glow and throb
Living in the ear

I hate the night
Pouring pools
Of black doubt

Filling the valleys
Of daylight
Making into memory
The Earth
Of the warming sun

I hate the night
Building blind
Upon the mind
Making reality
Of the black ooze
That lapped the swampy
Cambrian shore

I hate the night
But the stars...

Morning poem

I would that in the lighted dawn
When cold reality stalks the mind
The fiery portrait night has drawn
Does not appear as to the blind.

Let not the morning's rational
Erode the Passion of the heart
Or still the silent sighing swell
On mere pretence that we're apart

To think is why we are on Earth
To plan, to build, to sin
To feel is ours from our birth
To touch, to hold, to win

So why fight we the fated time
Or try to dam the flow
But to the lofty summit climb
And meet the warming glow.

Ace Restaurant – Espanola Ontario 1965

After school fries and coke
Second booth's where we spoke
Homework, gossip and her face
Are my memories of the Ace.

Icebergs in Trinity Bay (for a friend there)

Alack, great 'bergs ply o'shore
Witches brewed in Nordic realm
Somtin' foul is afoot I fear
While hands daliant hold our helm
And mewl and spew nonsense clear
We nash and dash o'r hill and dale
'til our own nature us impale.

Cleaning chalkboard erasers
Memories of the 1950s
SS4B Drury High Falls School

When the wonder day is done
With freedom near and in the sun
But it's then we do not balk
Watching teacher rest the chalk
Beside it then, on dusty rail
We see the two, the felts prevail
They lift the two with teasing smile
Scans the class, for little while
"Who..." they ask, who so sly
"Who will take these
Take and fly?"
Teasing more they hold them high.
"And out the door, but do not fall
"Whack erasers 'gainst the stuccoed wall"
"Me... me, me!" The cries ring out
Followed by the groan and shout
As Becky flies from her chair
Squeals so loud and grabs the pair
"Teacher's pet," is muttered low
But we defeated really know
One day soon will be our time
To glow in the thing sublime
For we know as we must
We'll soon breathe chalky dust.

Old note books

Give me a blank scribbler
A Hilory to climb
Fill with silly thoughts
Perhaps some sublime
Sharpened Venus pencils
Worn to the nub
As another idea
It would scratch as I would grub
Funny ink smudges
From fountain pen askew
Only the last page
A ball point it knew
Then hidden away in that old dusty drawer
Found by our children
When we be no more.

A beautiful new

Around each turn
Is a beautiful new
I no longer yearn
For this startling view
What I am seeing
Is the best of its kind
Vistas of eye
To capture my mind
Every new thing
That ruffles my way
Lives in my heart
'til a newer holds sway.

Australian Outback

Sun sits squarely
Down upon
This land
Harsh red stone
Clay
Pulped beneath
The fist
Ten million years
Spreading away
To nowhere
This alter
Where the death
Adder crawls
On its belly
In homage
And ribbed cow
Takes a meal
Five miles long
Rewarded
With a bellyful
Of bitter water
And man walks
Softly

10-2-72
In Sunda Straight December 1971

Where islands ride
That tropic air
The golden moon
Rising over Java
Let us be there
In its silence
Drinking the spiced night
Together

In Alice Springs 2-4-71

If I were Fiji bound
These feet no longer
On the ground
Desert dust no more
Upon my feet
This desire no more
Upon my heart
Some strange happiness
I would feel
Seeing the Suva stalls
Dark islanders
Haggling
Red-necked tourists
From the boat
And the green clad
Jungle hills
Children perfecting
That very first

English lesson
Chanting
"Give me money."
At the speeding
Tourist cars
Black-packed busses
The burning
Sunset sky
A much different song
Would I sing
If I were Fiji bound.

The Northland

North is where the cold wind blows
North is where the snow lies deep
North is where the skier goes
Where the hills are high and the slopes are steep

North is the land that's in the blood
To this patria the spirit loves
Through all the trials of fire and flood
We proudly return as ancient doves

This is the land that's rugged and bleak
Of stark grey rocks and fire
Where we may our fortune seek
Invade with wild desire

Well we come and plans we make
But with a sinister smile
Nature moves, our work reshapes
In just a little while

From south to north and north again
It stretches on and on
And since the ice it's just the same
Where we have never gone

We may come and dig and scar the land
And then move on again
But this expanse on which we stand
We shall never tame.

Memories in the heart
(for a friend who had suffered a great loss)

when the dawn is shining
in the valley of the sun
when good friends are taken
and it cannot be undone
through the tears and sadness
the future lived apart
all the finest memories
live still within the heart

Sonnet for Theresa

Lady in the mountain vale
Smiling sweetly on the dew
The worlds troubles quickly pale
Making all our spirits new
To her garden we do hasten
Trembling gently as we go
The sun itself is seen to chasten
Standing quiet in her glow
Sweet sweet berries she does offer
Giving all that we desire
From her Eden she doth proffer
Meeting all that we aspire
And when the day doth turn to night
We find calm within her light.

Theresa died in 2017

Water's Laughter

The laughter of water
Massaging stone
Lingering sunshine
Memory drifting home.
Rivers be mighty
Rolling to sea
Cutting down mountains
And rush to be free
But
The brook is playful
Trickling in fen
Quietly faithful
Beyond most, their ken
They be the place
Of child sized joy
Of frogs and snakes
For a little boy
Boot grabbing mud
And banks of green
Rocks and roots
In valleys mean
Playground of beaver
Muskrat too
With room for small feet
In their little zoo
While rivers carry
Cargo so fair
The creek holds memory
That always lives there.

Toronto 20-4-69

Feel this
Soft April pressed
Against the city
Sun gone
Revealing
This grey-blue sky
The neon's wink
Distance softens
Lighted windows stacked
Mercury vapour
Dotting fences
Across this
Black velvet world
Of Mary Jane
But
The siren screams
Echo
    Ing
Back
    From
The
    Towers
Of light
Winos cursing Sunday
Cops chasing whores
Belching black phalli
Crashing glass
And the monsters
Of Air Canada

Tempting me to
Wish the night
Without the damned
The city
Screams NO
Lights
Are turned on
By people

Ode to a snowy Toronto parking lot

Black flat shapeless plain
Smelling of monoxide
Concealed by dusty
City breath
You are no-man's-land
But fear not
You are blameless
We conceived you
Raping the Earth
Slapping on
Thick, stinking formless tar
Pounding it flat without fear
For Lumbrici cannot vote
And so with you we have created
An alter
To our chromed
Blood-thirsty idols
I would hate you
But tonight it is forbidden
Stronger powers than we
Hiding our folly

Have clothed you in loveliness
Albeit whore-like
Fitting you
Make believe princess
In argentine gown
But tomorrow
The clock strikes twelve
No silver slipper will remain
Then, I will hate you

Who? Me?

I'll smile at a picketer
Honk at a sign
But give up my driving?
You're out of your mind.

Dusk from the Sam McBride (1966)

The moon sits silent on the bay
Birds in flight dip and soar
Engines rumble from below
Overhead the reaction roar

Phosphorescence unites the sky
And lake into a hemisphere
Of lakers and sails to and fro
Lighted buoy and darkened pier.

The city, silhouetted soars
While abaft land lies low
Our wake becomes a turbid trail
Back to time we join the flow.

Hand on the wheel

A ship that flies
On a following wind
A hand of a friend
On the wheel
And turns to port
To a guiding light
And arms of love
To feel.

Brandi's thank you poem for her sailor friends
From the novel, Under Shadows

There be many a reef
And many a shoal
But fair freshening winds
And the north-star true
Will guide this vessel
Safe home with you

Morning's kiss

And day's fire
Consumes the earth
Night descending
Dark ,cold as char
But
Glowing once more
In morning's kiss.

Nature spun

And with a sigh
Lie
beneath the sun
feel
life in nature spun

Dance of life

Dance beneath the leafy green
Dance beneath the branches bare
Dance in the snowy meadow
Dance in the cooling dew
Dance beneath the moonlight
Dance for we and you

Internet protest

Ah irony, sarcasm allegory and wit
Metaphor and satire too
Let's assail the foe
With bow and quiver
Of literary might
That'll show the bastards
Just who's who, who's right

All must fall

Fight the great
Symbolic fight
Read and write

Upon the wall
Never mind
That words and wall
In the end
All must fall.

Eyes of a believer
From "The End of shadows" – Don Hayward 2014

I fear the stranger
I fear the danger
I fear the shadows of the night
I hide behind gates and bars
And never ever see the stars

Finally, we see

The young are learning
The old are remembering
The middle are too busy
To be
But when we last stand
Before star-studded land
We'll know and finally we'll see.

Welcome

Welcome
To the planned society
Of planned people
In planned disarray
Where everyone is organized
Living, loving, dying
To plan
Where everything occurs
In ministrated spontaneity
So that opposition
And position is the same
Ripples being born
With regulated random.

Ode to the Sixties
(Written Jan 1, 1970 in more optimistic times)

So we have parted
Leaving you behind
You sixties
Having described
The mandatory ten
Invisible arcs
Leaving the haunting
Sounds
Of the day
When once again
A cowboy patrolled
The lonely Texas plain
Scouting the way to hell
Of the screaming divisions

Dying in the swamps
Keeping us
From declaring war
Keeping us
From declaring peace
Of the whimpering babies
Forced into
Hot breeches of canon
To win dark pools
Of stinking oil
Black
As their own skin
Of the bullets
Hitting barbed wire
And warm bodies
Baking beneath graveyard dunes
Of the shouts
Beginning to rise above
The fire and faint
Tentative smiles
Behind the shouts
Of the masses
Singing loudly
Not battle hymns
But words of peace
Love and
All blood is red
Of the haunting
"Light's on!" cried
From a lonely outpost
In the night
As four eyes gazed
Upon that cosmic cinder

And the sound
Of a strong voice
Echoing across the world
Boiling up into tomorrow
Ringing
From a living grave
"I have a dream!"

Reflections On Apollo 11

So we have
Thought our way
Out of the cradle
Our being expanding
On fiery fingers
Pointing out
Towards the stars
Melting away
The much cursed
Chains of Earth

Our spirit soars
As it did
When once we crawled
Upon our bellies
Out of the stinking
Cambrian soup
As it did
When once we stood
Upon the clinging clay
First saw stars

So now standing

Upon our cradle's edge
Trembling
In plastic boots
Poised to fling
Ourselves away
Let us throw back
The cradle's sheet
Our secret self
Has soiled
To leave this bed
Soft and warm
Against our safe return

Cosmos

I look about
This oasis of life
And see many trees
Beneath which are
Many conversations
Ernest and true no doubt
Important and beyond
My understanding
So I turn away
To watch the boy
Scaling the date palm
Beyond
The camel drover
Struggling through the dust
Leading his beasts, his life
To water and refreshing rest
Beyond
The restless desert itself

In hummocks and hollows
Seared beneath the sun
Sand restless on the wind
Hiding
Our mysterious future
Beyond the sky

To Vega

Bosom friend
Standing silent
And alone
In the Cyclops's head
Crying
Timid little tears
Then blinking
Gone

Humans
Written for Mary P.

Nothing under the sun
Always the sun alone
Nothing under the moon
Always the moon alone
Nothing under the Earth
Always the Earth alone
Nihil sub sol
Semper sol solus
Nihil sub luna
Semper luna sola
Nihil sub terra
Semper terra sola

The others
(Footnote to the social register)

Perhaps they are
As some have said
Vulgar
Using curses
For punctuation
Spitting
In the dust
Swilling
Cheap beer

I have seen them
They are so
But
At times
When their eyes soften
Speaking of their youth
I realize
These too are men

The End to My Hunting

I feel the sunlight
warm against
these corroding autumn hills
the leaves
brilliant and dying
cooling winds
sneaking
amongst the rocks
felling
the corpses of summer
stuffy damp
this decaying deadfall
where I sit
a proud pine
before the fire
the gun
twenty gauge but
grown heavy
now broken
lying mutely
against my perch
laminar trails
of smoke
drifting downwind
away to nothingness
from my blasted briar
from below
where the broad basin
half mile square
spreads out
rimmed harshly

with grey
northern granite
the echo drums
upon both my ears
a grouse
calling his mate
I have shot

Rock cut on Highway 17 from the high school bus

I passed this place
Many times by car
Or packed and darkened bus
So knew it well enough
To have pointed a finger
Saying that's the place
|If I had remembered it

Once to change
A tire, a belt, or hose
This place became a stop
With uncut weeds becoming flowers
Common drab granite machine-split friends
And happy shade
Old and natural pine
This place became a friend
A secret part of me
So that always
I pass this place
Now
And then

Wild Flower Time Exposure

Why are you
Hiding
Upon this barren
Winter-blasted hill
Among rock-moss
And clinging
Windswept lichen
The ice of spring
Glistening
On bare granite

Unrivaled are you
In Ottawa's
Symmetrical grandeur
The Gorge's rim
And
Everyone's backyard

Growing
Not because
You are bedded
Washed and choked
In sheep's manure
But because
You are
Infinity deciding so
Ten billion years
Before
When your atoms
Were in a star

An Earthly king
In a cosmic
Game of draughts
Built block
By block
Move
By move
As the universe
Challenged itself

Told to grow
In sterile
Transient Sand
Resting
On its way
To the sea

To grow for
Our pleasure
But not by
Us

Experimental biology

Testing one two; testing one two
We're mankind, that's what we do
Strutting on stage to get it right
And if we do we'll last the night.

Ripples in the dark

When out of the east
That golden glow
An hour past the loss of the moon
When the night begins to swoon
And expectation is all we know
Then all ripples in the dark
The thoughts, dreams, fears
And blazing brands of night
Become remote as cedar stands
Haunting, in bare foreign lands
They died, die, will die as the night
So to as all that never truly lives
But by being some small service gives
Even death creates true life
Being to it
As the stone, the knife.

Thoughts on a damaged washroom wall

Cries for help
Need not be
Screams in the night
Or elegant poetry
But simple acts we see
Quietly desperate
In private
And these fractures left
Be all we see.

Coronation 2023

It seems this day
To give a thought about this king
Opine in deep and sonorous tone
Of he who sits on blooded throne
The latest in the pomp and strut
Even tho he said, oh what?
His own opine on the day
A man who's not to have a say
How dare he do, oh he should
Have smiled meek and quiet stood
So this day trumpets tone
As he sits his arse on stolen scone
Neath jewelled cap and ermine white
Shoulder burdened by epaulet bright
As shouts and song fill the hall
Pretending there was no empire fall
Standing in symbolic plight
Of empire lost of all its might
It seems this day

To give a thought about this king
Seems a silly and an empty thing

Silly

The origins of the English language

English historic
Is English hysteria
With words so mal
It seems like malaria

Don't let your lingo
In alleys dark lurk
For the English Billy-jack
Will steal and smirk

Your words that belong
In sunnier climes
Twisted and bent 'neath
Big Benny chimes

So drawn and fiddled
They linger along
In London fog
Where they ne'er belong.

I'm in a stew

I'm in a stew
If I only knew
I was in a stew
I'd know I was a dumpling
Gooey, round and white
And laugh and splash in gravy
Until that final bite.

ABM Dialogue

"Cluck, cluck," said the Duck
"Cluck, cluck, indeed," said Grandma Goose
"What are you?"
"Some kind of chicken?"
"Cluck, cluck,: said the Duck.

Banshee Blarney

There's a Banshee in my chimney
I heard her there last night
She howled and wailed and screamed at me...
No!   I know I wasn't tight!

I was lying down for slumber,
To catch a wink or two
It startled me like thunder
As it whistled down the flue.

I lit a fire beneath her
To try and drive her off,
But it didn't work, I tell you sure
The damned howl became a cough!

Oh there's a Banshee in my chimney
I heard her there last night,
She howled and wailed and screamed at me ...
But I don't think that I was tight!

The noise was really terrible
I can tell you, goodness knows
And though my mother's Irish

I got the garden hose.

Well first I tried it upwards
To spray her from below
But called her rather nasty words
When the soot began to flow.

Well I'm stubborn as a mule
Even when as black as coal
And though I looked the fool
I had set myself a goal.

I gained the roof in finer style
Than Sir Hillary, so I'm told
And though it took a little while
It was something to behold

The hose was gaily squirting
Much water, maybe more
But with the Banshee flirting
I forgot the kitchen floor

Well my wounds really pain me
From the wife propelled chair
And what about the Banshee?
Please, the question isn't fair!

Oh there's a Banshee in my chimney
I heard her there last night
She howled and wailed and screamed at me ...
Well ... maybe a little tight!

Spaghetti Squash Dinner

Rope in a boat
With a meatball crew
Sailed at supper time
It couldn't float
But we must here note
The taste was quite sublime.

Don't come for dinner
A little dash of Ogden Nash

If you're going to meet
A meat-eating dinosaur
Better to meet 'im
After he's eaten
So you he won't.

Winter? Who knows?

Winter will be frightful
I guess
With snows and blows
Freezing cheeks and toes
But when?
I go with the fuzzy-wuzzies
Rather than those two farmers
Al n' Mac

Winter leaves in a huff

Winter knocked on my back door
Cap in hand, he said.
"Sorry my going's late and lean
But I've left a drift by the shed"
He turned to go, stopping then
And blew a cold breath on me
Spring is sprung I feel her now
And the birdies are in the tree.

In light of the scarding moon

and the scary bargs snitched
in the grumbug tree
neath the scarding moon
ink-nigh eyes
dreary darkness skyes
lighted by the groon

Stoned at the Henge

Druid Druid on the mall
Or is it bell
And candle call?
Through the mists
'tis hard
to see at all
When King shall rise
And King shall fall.

Sis

A sister is, sometimes
A person, to be sure
But just in case you're wondering
They are someone to endure

At times they're cute and cuddly
Sweet as a summer rose
Next they are tigers clawing
With fangs of cutting prose

I speak with some authority
See the scared face and limb
But if the universe were offered
I wouldn't trade her in
So take your gold and frankincense
And all your prized myrrh
And don't you dare insult her name
Or you may hear her purr.

The Ballad of Cousin Sue
(Or, the not so silent listener)

Oh come you all, you men of heart
You men so bold and true
Heed this warning I impart
For I sing of Cousin Sue.

Well she is a fair young girl
With eyes of smiling blue
And hair so fine and not a curl
But beware of Cousin Sue.

For Sue is of the female kind
With all their whiles and ways
I pity now the poor man blind
Who loves her in coming days

For when about with lovely Sue
Trying to turn her heart
She'll ask a question, maybe two
And give no chance to start.

"Oh, what is this?" and "Who is that?"
"Where and what are you?"
"Do you think I'm beautiful?"
"Oh, please me, tell me true."

Take note for you must answer her
Take note you must reply
Answer right and answer quick
Another question's nigh.

So tell her she is beautiful
It's easy and you would
For when you see my Susie
You'll know you really should.

And just when you despair for her
Thinking she's a tease
She'll ask, "Do you love me?"
"Answer if you please."

But when you speak tell her true
Don't break her golden heart
For I have answered, "Yes, I do."
Her defender is my part.

That's the tale of Susie
Or all I know so far
But then again my cousin
Is like the summer star.

For men will chart their course by her
(Though some will come to grief)
One will have her warming heart
To her, give up his life.

The Broadcasting Blues
(If like me you are older than dirt, CBC censorship of This Hour has Seven Days 1966.)

The C.B.C. has more for me
Than weather and news not old
But conflict and drama in Cinerama
And Quixotic actions bold

Watson and Leiterman and LaPierre
Were roaring and ready to go
But the men at the head nearly dropped dead
And good old Alphonse said no

Quote the courageous three: "For the public we
For their good we won't back down."
But management said, "We're at the head
By God we wear the crown."

The battle raged, "We won't be caged!"
Cried the three is chorus fine
"If that is wished, you won't be missed."
Said the Board to keep in time.

The Commons was roaring; tempers were soaring
Poor Judy just couldn't cope
As belligerent forces spurred on their horses
And each took a little more rope

And now you see on management tree
Swing our heroes to-and-fro
What's the response of good old Alphonse?
He wished they were down below

Now there a caper called White Paper
Something the brass should know
For re-organization and regimentation
Would deal them quite a blow

The last I looked our goose was cooked
As we public just can't win
So let's sit still off of the grill
Change channels away from the din

Overripe bananas

But what of old-banana bread
Its flavour of curved and bent conception
Me thinks of cakes in cups
Wrought with thick tropic taste
Quickly devoured
That they will nay tomorrow
Suffer today's banana's fate

Uncertainty

Cat in a hat
I fancy that
Cat in some socks
Or cat with a fox
A swingy cat door
With fancy cat locks
But no never no never
No never no nox
Would I ever believe
A cat in a box.

One too many

Felix asked many questions
Ten to be exact.
So now you know
After the last ...
Where the cat is at.

A present from Gizmo the cat

I caught a wee mouse
Right here in the house
And took it beside your bed
At four or near
When I knew you would hear
I crunched up its poor wee head.

Puppy

Slobbery puppy
Licks my face
When we move
We always race
"Let me in
Let me out
I only whine
I never shout
When I scramble
About your feet
You know I want
A tasty treat
My brown eyes stare
My nose will shove
And give you all
Unending love."

For Usayan friends who come late to Thanksgiving

May your black Friday be black
Because you're sleeping instead
All snuggle and burping and farting in bed
May the box stores go broke
At your indolent sloth
Though the patriots fan you
With their stripy, star cloth.
So eat up and drink down
All over your town
May your turkey be hot
And your gravy quite brown.

Isotopia

because i be yeller
i'm not going to teller
the names of the dopes
who named isotopes
of hydrogen

it was a big gang
who made a big bang
when with great hopes
they sliced isotopes
of uranium

then did some neat trix
added lithium six
having some fun
a neat little sun

of fusium

now back in the past
these folks had a blast
no bit of repent
they made element
one thirteenium

where did they go
no one would know
perhaps they sup
sipping a cup
of deuterium

A thing or two

The thing is this
And this other thing too
So now that we've discussed
A thing or two
Lets on with fun
At the human zoo
Where bigger is better
Goes the marketing moo
The thicker the steak
The better the chew
But don't eat the fat
And never the lean
For the bovines eat
More grass than we've seen
But we won't heed
The shouting Green Team
So soon the human is
Will turn to a been

Serious

Chapter one

After opening
The book
Perhaps tearing
The dust jacket
Just a bit
It stares
Into your face
And dares you
Read beyond
For it is
The supreme piece
And holds its status well
'I am first!'
It mocks
'Better
than the rest
to read at all
you must pass
through me.'
But beware
For onliness is best
Supported
By little else
Than ink stained
Polluted paper
That somehow missed
Incineration

"I am like a book ... "- Christopher Isherwood

The Library

I entered a room
Whose walls were made of words
Etched upon the ghosts of trees
Arranged in neat rows
Precise and deliberate
Cleverly met and mixed
Neatly stitched into tales
Conceived in wild imagination
Crafted to many a purpose
Poured from tortured souls
Or knitted by avarice mind
Seducing my being
Clamouring upon my brain
A thick confusing cacophony
Yet strangely silent
With their backs to the sun.

A book is to read

Or tear the covers open,
stare wide eyed
at the author's sweat,
the book binds words that will out;
thoughts; ideas; longings; questions; answers; fun and satisfaction.
Return it to the shelf well used,
tattered, corners bent and smudged
and stained and torn.
And again and again until

The thing rests
limply in its place
handy and still beaconing
calling you to the rocky shore of the joy
of its beginning and once again
the satisfying disappointment
of its end.

Infinite Intricacy

Shaded forest paths
filled with dancing shadows and
pungent smells of life and death;
high hills washed
with gentle summer breeze
overlook the broad green valley;
rocky shores where
lapping of waves reminds
eternity is today
folded upon itself
in infinite intricacy

Healing

Take me to the forest
Let me fall in love with
The sights, smells, sounds and
Feeling of the place
The shades and flashes
Cries, rustling
Soft moaning of the wind
Then let me sit upon a stone
Taking this grandeur in

Closing my eyes
Absorbing its spirit
Taking my spot in the eternity
Of which this place
Is but the latest form

Sorry Karl
In praise of the naked ape

Perhaps we are
As some have said
Advanced
For indeed
Do we not
Turn
Night into day
Whisper
A million miles
Speed
Over, on and under
The Earth

We may
Push a button
And with only slight delay
A city explodes
Half a world away

I think back
When we
The naked ape
First left the tree
Took an antelope bone

And broke it
Over our neighbour's skull

I must agree
We are advanced
Having made great progress
Improving the club

Sonnet XI

When I venture to think on it
Life is self-defeating madness
Little else but man made sadness
Hardly worth a song or sonnet
Why then should I dwell upon it
When wars are made without redress
And man's actions do regress
To pillage and destroy by habit
But isn't like something more
Than birth and suffering and painful end
Where all people live a lie
We must not reject the lore
That long since past ages send
To lose all hope is but to die.

Sonnet XII

I ask you all, we fools of time
Here as we grovel in the slime
Were we born but to live and die
Or does our hope in the future lie
Surely this world cannot be

Our ultimate end, our destiny
When cruel corruption and coldness of heart
Smother all good or it greater part
There must be more beneath the pain
Of fathers and sons and daughters we've slain
Than acres of swamp bought with blood
And bones that rot entombed in mud
Let us search and work someday
To find the light, the peaceful way

Ode to Yesterman 6-8-69

You
Who do not search
Are the dead
Long years ago
You lived
Dead
Feeling long
Your sunset slow
Walking into
The east at dusk
But you loved
Your children then
Pointing these on
Towards the east
And now
Short painful dawn
Tickles the darkness
Your children's faces
Catch the glow
Of your death
And see the east

Summer 1972
Downwind from the Espanola Kraft mill

There was a time
A fence
All that
Was needed
To keep you
Safe
For sure a cow
One morning might
Break through
So that you went
To your neighbour
Saying
She ate a half
Day's grass
He answering
Yes, so
We are even
You agree remembering
Last year
Your cow
But
Today when sulphuric
Morning breezes
Choke you
To wakefulness
There is no
Friendly neighbour
Who eats your smoke
All you can do
Is fight.

Ode to the leaning birch on the Spanish River far bank

Look at that tree on the darkening shore
Leaning over the rivers roar
As horizontal as we could do
Drawn with pencil and straight edge true
For a teacher's: "Not perfect, but that will do."
Those without much river lore
Might scoff and sniff and sometimes roar:
"What a lazy useless thing,
That can't stand straight or anything."
But let me sit on this near bank,
Amongst struggling saplings and punkie dank,
To think as I have for years gone by
What a thing it is to try
Watching this birch live on
Given its niche as natures pawn
With the choice to live or die
We see what living life will try
A little seedling decides to stay
And fight as long as its roots felt clay
For years we've watched it there abide
Through winter's cold and spring's high tide
To me a legend, a friend for sure
A lesson of life, but to endure.

Day's End

And when my hands,
Wearied from the work
Rest upon the top rail
Gazing over the shadowed
Forms of beasts
Contemplating the setting sun
Angry warning sky
Or perhaps promising
If I think at all
I think of the need
And meaning, and work
Then longing for the natural
Pursuit of the white tail
Fiddlehead and leek
Wild in the cooling restful shadows
Of the forest
Joking by the evening fire
Balancing new generations
Upon my knee
With sparks reaching for the purpling sky
Then finding rest with the birds
Amongst the night-time chorus
Until the sun gently calls us,
"Once more, repeat the quest."

The four horses

Four shadowed horses
Stand midst the trees
Breathing mist and fire
Into cold, night air
Riders crouch beside
Waiting
Chortling
Breath rasping, coughing
Teeth gnashing hungrily
Stone grating on steel
A pale, ghostly hand
Reaching from the dark
Grasping at the neck
Of humanity

Blud Red Moon

The hammer's blow
Met the forge's glow
Beneath the blud red moon
Four horses stood
In the shadowed wood
Beneath the blud red moon
Fiery eyed
Their riders cried
Beneath the blud red moon
They rode the night
With fearsome might
Beneath the blud red moon
Anguished cries
Filled the skies

Beneath the blud red moon
And dawn was hid
By the work they did
Beneath the blud red moon.

Creeping Death
(My first serious poem written as a Grade 10 project for Mrs. Sparling, Copper cliff High 1962)

The moon is down; the night is late
Now come the men, full of hate
Slinking and sliding
Creeping and hiding
Riding their cart of death

Crawling and slipping into their hole
They carry their cargo of death
And out through the wall
Looping and winding
Twisting and turning
They lay their road of death

Now around they turn and away they run
'til none are left, save just one
He is bent, his body still, and then
Flickering and flashing
Spitting and sparking
Goes the death of other men

It slowly travels that stinking tunnel
Until, at last it reaches the muzzle
And then, up to the top
Writhing and twisting
Climbing and flinging

Goes the death of other men

And now as the first grey light of dawn
Streaks the eastern sky
There the bodies of other men lie
Who no longer live to die
For that stinking, spitting flame of death
Came at them from below
A laid them dead, the other men
The men we never know.

When I submitted this to the Espanola High yearbook, the teachers thought I was suicidal or something and interviewed me.

Young or old, soldiers die
(For my father-in-law, and friends Ron and Art)

When in later years
Burden gently falls from grasp
Their tears no longer flow
They ease into eternity
With comrades long fallen
Beneath sand
Blooded
By friend and foe
As they lie
Comforted by liberating sleep
We must sigh
In quiet humility
Vow never again to cry havoc
Never send our children
To die in horror
Fast or slow.

No glory

Battle glory
Lives in story
Where blood is spilt
All red
But in the real
Clash of steel
Their blood is spilt
'til dead

Remember

They walked not
A road of glory
But the harsh path
Of sacrifice
Yes embrace their courage
Their suffering, their loss
Remember, remember
But especially their warning
Let only the flower
Be blood red.

More mothers weeping

The eleventh
of the eleventh
of the eleventh
A clock's tick
Picked in vanity
By generals and kings

Thus before the guns
Were silent
Left more blood
Upon the ground
More mothers weeping
Replaced
The battle sound

Never more

When boys shall grow
From their mother's arm
And sail away to soldier
For the dollar or the crown
And never more to tread
The soothing sod of home
Or touch the lips
That loved, and sleep alone.

Bravely off to war

What is the greater value
Medals, flashing in the sun
Pinned to coats of surge
Over hearts broken by the gun?
Or is it the memory of a boy
Marching bravely off to war
When banners flew
Hats raised high
Amidst the cheering roar?
Or is it his memory of
The days so fearful real
When his new friends fell beside

Amidst mud and blood and steel?
Leaving memories in his head
That never still nor heal?
Or is it cold November days
We stand before a stone
Pretending there is glory in
The sin we can't atone?
Peacefully those boys now lie
Now silenced is the pain
And forgotten in a drawer
Are the medals, just the same.

Master's grip

When I survey events unfold
When men of comfort
Strut so bold
Mouthing the puppet's lying script
Strings all hidden
Beneath master's grip
Proclaiming love for foreign mud
For it to shed
Young men's blood.
We slaves will die, they do not care
Will spend our lives
To grow their share.

2-4-71

love
life
leading
life
love
overing
undering
othering
some
one
where
how
time
again
then
now
time
hate
life
end
life
aim
click
bang
end
me
you
all

1-1-70

When the gavel
Is larger than the man
It turns
With concentrated
Slow deliberation
Straining sound muscle
Forcing the man
To thinking, feeling
Its weight
Requiring just cause
To move it
Up, and down
When the gavel
Is small
Resting easily
In any hand
It squeaks
A hollow thoughtless rapping
Upon a table
As imperfect as itself
As though pretending
It were not so
It becomes
A mere hammer
Crude and cruel
And punishing
Bruising soft mettle
Forcing all
Too easily
Into rough
Detroit forms

Fitting the mold
Of the man
Quiet
But full of pain

One and one

I listened
To a revolutionary
Yesterday
Dressed as he was
In his peasant costume
Though
What do peasants wear
These days

He spoke of Marx
And Lenin and Mao
Proudly showing
An autographed
Red-bound book
With earnest eyes
Full of future promise

He spoke of Che
Freedom and universities
And democracy
Though a bullet
Is still the best ballot
Reactionaries
Will soon be voted out
The beauty of life
Personal dignity

And man's right
To live for himself
Beyond the fear
Of death
And perhaps
After all
A reactionary
Is not a man

The common man
Passed by
Was he happy
With his wife fat
And children healthy
He shrugged
And went on his way

He does not know
Said my revolutionary
That he should care
The rich
Are rich
And he is not
We must teach him
That he is unhappy
I must make war
Destroy the wealthy
Why, I asked
Why
It will make
The common man
Happy
End all war

After all
I am a revolutionary
Bearing the truth
And believing
In the integrity
Of my profession

I listened
To a reactionary
Yesterday
Dressed as he was
In robes
And chain of office
Though what clothes power
These days

He spoke of Churchill
And Buckley and Louis XIV
Proudly showing
His degrees
And directorships
With earnest eyes
Telling of prosperity

He spoke of Burke
Freedom and universities
And democracy
Though a bullet
Is still the best ballot
Revolutionaries
Will soon be voted out
The beauty of life
Personal dignity

And man's right
T live for himself
Beyond the fear
Of death
And perhaps
After all
A revolutionary
I not a man

The common man
Passed by
Was he happy
With his wife fat
And children healthy
He shrugged
And went on his way

He does not know
Said the reactionary
That he should care
The revolutionaries
Threaten our position
We must teach him
He is happy
I must make war
Destroy
The revolutionaries
Why, I asked.
Why
It will make
The common man
Happy
End all war

After all
I am a leader
Bearing the truth
And believing
In the integrity
Of my profession

Where is my cross?

My duty done
I shut
And bolt the door
Where pigeons
Gobble up
My stale crumbs
Of bread

And so now
I
May turn
To live my life
To smile loudly
Over my act
Of Christian charity

Hidden carbon

Mother Nature swept her carbon
Beneath her well-spun rug
It'll be there millions of years
She said laughing with a shrug

I'm busy making bees and birds
And nice smelling little flowers
Then I'll make a bipedal thing
Who all these things devours.

Perhaps I'll lift the corner
Of my carbon hiding rug
Just to watch the biped smirk
As it eats it like a drug.

But if it burns the carbon quick
Making house and rug to fall
I'll bring back those old acid bugs
It won't bother me at all.

Our carbon didn't sink

Oh, for the olden days
When winter was no surprise
When cold and snow blew on the wind
Right before our eyes.
Before the climate caught a fever
Because our carbon didn't sink
Cold and heat and dry and wet
It's enough to make you think.

Oh Jordan

Oh Jordan
Fickle and flowing
Let me enfold thee
Use you up
And make you mine
I will defend your bones
With armies and might
And tho I kill you
It is my right.

Try not my faith

Burden me not
With facts and truth
Try not my faith
Solid from my youth
Let me drift
On the starlit sea
Ignoring the tsunami
Coming for me.

Storm Cloud

Blackened spectre in the west
Come! Put me to the test
Though we know
That man is best
Rumble…
So you growl
I have no fear
Still that hollow voice
I hear
And rumble still…
You are a puffed
And empty thing
Yet you dare
The gauntlet fling?
And rumble still…
Come not here
My power is great
And you won't dare
Attract my hate
And rumble still…
I am man
And on this Earth
By God I take
My place as first
And rumble still…
Away with you
And all your kin
To flout my word
Is grievous sin
And rumble still…
So you are here

I laugh aloud
There is no fear
From a puffed up cloud
And rumble…

Spider

Brown and ugly
Deadly perhaps
Friendly
To others
Of your kind
Wandering
This hallway
With care
Cringing
In corners
With fear
As the two
Footed giant
Passes
Too large
To be real
Or to care
You let him
Pass
But nudging
Aggressive toe
Calls you out
Reacting with
Your ancestor's
Instinct
You attack

The giant belly
Feels sudden fear
But noting
Your courage
Moves back
Into his own
Universe
Leaving you
Alive
Brown and ugly
Deadly perhaps
Friendly
To others of
Your kind
But in his room
Noting your courage
Would crush you

I sold my soul

You blow 16 tons
And what do you get?
Another day warmer
Or deeper in wet.
St Peter don' you call me
I can't go
I sold my soul to the corporate store.
I was born one morning
Boy the sun, did shine
But I picked up a shovel
And dug me a mine
I loaded 16 tons

Thought it would last
So I crawled on home
And had me a blast.
You blow 16 ton
And what do you get?
Another day warmer
Or deeper in wet.
St Peter don' you call me
I can't go
I sold my soul to the corporate store.
When you see it coming
Better step aside
A lot of folks won't
And a lot will die.
The oceans are dying
Feel their pain?
I sold my soul
For a wee bit of gain.
You blow 16 ton
And what do you get?
Another day warmer
Or deeper in wet.
St Peter don' you call me
I can't go
I sold my soul to the corporate store.
The air is toxic
The winds are big
We ain't got long
On this industrial gig
Either momma will come
And smack us down
Or we'll smarten up
And get out of town.

You blow 16 ton
And what do you get?
Another day warmer
Or deeper in wet.
St Peter don' you call me
I can't go
I sold my soul to the corporate store.

Profits

A child stepped
In front of a dollar
Speeding on its way
To company profits
The Queen smiled
No less
So I'm told
Though the child died
"Was all her fault"
Said the company
Said the government
Said the court
"We are not murders."
Said the company
And declared a profit
"We are not grave diggers"
Said the workers
And declared a war
Whereupon the company
Became the workers
Whereupon the profits
Became the people
And no longer killed.

But…

"If wishes were horses
Beggars would ride."
If words were bullets
Our masters would hide.
Alas neither one
Is real, you see
So beggars must crawl
And we are not free.

We dig deep

Give me back what is mine
Said nature with a shrug
Stop your petty squealing
It's your own grave you have dug

Tomorrow's Dawning

So Adam
You are lodged
In this cell
These many years
The scaffold's shadow
Crossing your doorstep
Industriously making noises
And scrawling
Meaningless markings
Upon these
Decaying walls
While out
In the full sunlight

Of the day
Your noose
Is being prepared
The first coil
Wound
By your own hand
From innocent purpose
Perhaps
But taught and firm
Just the same
And over the ages
Your kindly
Intelligent brothers
Have tied and
Retied the snaking loop
Until not even
Your kindly
Intelligent brothers
Can undo
This supreme piece
Of their craft
For you damned
Your children
By etching in gold
What we hath wrought
Let no god put asunder

Mausoleum

Laying brick on the endless wall
Laying brick 'til the sun will fall
Laying brick in the killing sun.
Laying brick 'til the course is done

When we were young

when we were young
and not so very
long ago when
the winter did not
sit upon the land
but came flaunting
settling amongst the spruce
waiting silently five months
in the cedar swamp
for the sun's memory

when we were young
and not so very
long ago when
the bush stopped
the pine rested
cold and quiet
only shattered but little
when we stood in awe
as Dad's axe cut
and echoed and splintered
a tree for Christ
praying with our
excitement and hope
then leaving the others
sleeping silently, alone

when we were young
and not so very
long ago when
touch and smile

kept us safe
and we were not alone
when we were young
and not so very long ago

metal pounding metal
supposed controlled explosions
did not mock
nor torment the great sleep
did not pretend
that we were hardy
or stronger than cold
beneath six layers
of bull feathers
and only so long
as the machine works

when we are old
and not so very
long away when
the machine will not
strut upon the land
but wait silently
in the swamp
stopped cold and quiet
by the memory

A Night On the Trail

(Robert Service slept here)

The howl of the winter wind
Lingers mournful in the trees
Hear the banshee wail
On the northern trail
Your blood begins to freeze

The wolf is out there in the night
It's his mocking voice you hear
You know him well
He was bred in hell
You tremble with the fear

The northern lights stage running fights
The trees they sway and groan
You fed the fire
It roars higher
And you're a little less alone.

The stars are silent sentries
Above fields of silver snow
And with their gleam
You start to dream
Of loved ones long ago.

The world long gone silent
A voice, eyes, softening hair
Shed silent tears
For yester-years
A heart once filled with care.

The night speeds swiftly onward
And darkness turns to dawn
With a weary heart
You make your start
For the trail travels on.

North

Beneath the numb
November air
Staring trees
Blasted bare
Dusting snow
Fleeting falls
The pale moon
Owl calls
Whispering wind
Sweeping rock
Testing well
Winter's lock
Spirits' land
Spirits' face
Scored beneath
The season's race
Demanding man
Holy writ
Once staying, being
Part of it.

Childish Memory (December 24, 1967)

Tonight
I saw the shadow
Of a child's face
Many miles
Many moons
Ago

I saw ...
Remembering
And with that memory
Cried

Lost was the day
When last I cried
Lost with my faith
And illusions
Of the world

But I cried
The hot tears
Flowing back
Through the paths
Of loneliness until
All my life was now

The blue of water
Summer green
Grey granite
Moon-silvered snow

The joy

Of a speechless friend
The sorrow
Of a dog's golden body
Stiff and cold
Upon a bare wood floor

The cement of my cornerstone
Crumbled
And all of me that was
Safely locked away
Poured out
Choking my senses

We are the past
Facing tomorrow
But sometimes
Seeing the shadow of yesterday
We must cry.

High Falls memories

It was a day
Shrouded in fog
Winter threatening in the hills
Of urgency, fear and hope
Of expectation
It was a day
When I was born

It was a day
Cold and bleak
Ice covered ground
Snowdrifts and struggle
Going to visit grandpa
It was a day
Perhaps it was his last

It was a day
Ice hard and smooth
Thrill and elation
Wind scrubbing faces
With cold and wild air
It was a day
Of winter crystal clear

It was a day
Of spring upon the hill
Wintered deer grazing
On warming hopeful slopes
Rivers on the road
It was a day
Rubber boots abound

It was a day
River flowing high and fast
Fascination and fear
Roaring rumble unseen
But flotsam and foam
It was a day
That fills a memory deep

It was a day
Sun dappling through the trees
Filled with laughter
Children gathered near
Friends and family playing
It was a day
That fills a child's year

It was a day
Children exploring on the hill
Adventure and fun
Scuffed shoes and skinned knees
Treasures found
It was a day
Knowing home was near

It was a day
Schoolbooks all bound
Trepidation and hope
Windows opening upon the world
Falling short but striving high
It was a day
Of ringing bells

It was a day

Autumn winds fresh upon the hill
Ending and beginning
Colour rioting over all
River waiting in the sun
It was a day
Where ice has just become

It was a day
Deep silent sleep
Cracking twigs beneath our feet
Morning sun that does not warm
Snow cold
It was a day
All time has run

It is a day
Memories run abound
Filling the long lost days
With family and friends now gone
But lingering deep within
This heart
Forever bound.

Humility

When you touch this frail hand
And lift me up, beyond
My rightful goal
And thus I search
Into your piercing eyes
To find in their darkness
Your cosmic soul

To then feel my own
Humble place
In that embracing eternity

Farewell to a love lost
Love is never lost c 1967

Do not fear for me
Love is not a trap
Though yes it hurts
Now and then, again
You know it all
(perhaps too well)

It is a lasting thing
Does not die within
Only if exploited
Ripped fully out
Its empty space is filled
With equal passion – hate

But do not fear
For love with care, removed
Though not returned remains
Transformed out of passion
Into knowing complete
Only warm where fire once lived
Not destroyed but not destroying
Eternal echoes of happiness
Enriching newer love

Do not fear for me
The goal was worth

Each drop of desire lost
Risks were not so great
To tame the try
What was found was love
Worthy in itself and
This, not pain, is savoured
No trap but echo
Enriching newer love

Do not look at me
Through your past
Nor let that pain
Destroy your tomorrow
I lived it too
She was not you
I am not the same

Do not see yourself
Through your past
Nor let that pain
Destroy your tomorrow
Risks are not so great
The goal is worth
Each drop of desire

Tread not

Tread not lightly on the land
Tread not at all.
Let the wild places be
Never suffer, fear or see
Our dreaded foot to fall.

A time that is no more

There was a time
That is no more
When moonbeams lit
A constant shore
But the rising
Waves do roar
Higher, higher
Now they soar
Rally hard against
Cliff and dune
Changing safety
Into ruin.

Dream time

I dream of a world
Where all of the houses
Have floors of mud
Or at least stone
Or hand hewn wood

I dream of a world
Where all of our hands
Know the feel of corn tassels
Drawn through
Not for harvest but for joy

I dream of a world
Where full throated bird song
Rouses us from sleep
Our own morning song

Rising in completing joy

I dream of a world
Where our struggle to reap
To occupy our space
Matches all other species
Struggles to create their bounty

I dream of a world
Where all living things
And the water and the air
Even the rock itself
Exist in mutual consideration

I dream of a world
Where the thunder of the skies
The thunder of the seas
The thunder of the river joining both
Shouts joy, love and eternity.

As we pass

Ending
Is beginning
Beginning
Is ending
Infinity
A closed ellipse
Of space and time
We are bare
Footprints
In the damp
Elliptical beach

The water here
Hides our mark
Higher we must go
To the dry dunes
And there leave
Ourselves
Ever safe
From eroding
Tides of time
But even here
The bated breath
Of ages
Hides our passing
Though no foot alike
All treads the same
In shifting sands of time

So we must
Gather stones
Make cement
Build there
A temple to ourselves
Scribing on
Look, I passed this place
So some may heed
Offering thanks
To our marking of the way

At day's end

At day's end when shadows fall
Soft comfort from sunbaked road
Obscuring all but rising stars
Glistening in your eyes, the memory
And as my life reaches for eternity
My being finds solace, resting
In your memory's grasp

Other meanderings in prose by Bristlehead.

The name, Bristlehead is a holdover from university in the 1960s and a long gone girlfriend.

I had a brush cut when I started university because that was the only hair style Dad could do. Money was short in my youth.

Don 1965

Mailboxes

Bits of humour I once sent to the Shelburne paper.

Greetings from down the line

Dear Editor,

Now that the leaves have fallen, animals in the barn, wood in the shed, the thoughts of all of us out in the countryside turn to one thing ... mail boxes!

A sure sign that winter approaches is found in the activity at lane's end as we frantically prepare for the attack of the most dangerous of winter beasts, the snowplough.

Amateur psychologists (are there professionals?) can seize the opportunity to discover their neighbour's attitude to life.

There is the defensive type, frantically applying florescent tape and painting the box bright yellow, or the traditional bright orange in Jessopville. The cynics among us ask: "Why give the plough driver a better target?"

Life's innovator rises to the challenge by devising a "plough proof" installation. This foolish crowd splits into two basic types. The first are mechanical engineers who hang the box on the end of a cantilevered structure of pipe and wire. These are designed to swing out of the way when hit. Of course, this leads to a contest among the drivers to see who can spin the thing all the way around. The second type is the ballistics expert who mounts the box upon a pole in a pail of dirt, designed to be thrown clear by the blade. First prize goes to the driver who wings it over the line fence with the most damage.

Our aggressive type wants to get even, erroneously believing that the plough can be taught a lesson. The less subtle of these spend much of their time trying to convince the Township that a two-ton bolder is the ideal mailbox post. More clever ones present devices such as welded four-inch chain mounted in concrete. Supposedly decorative, this artefact is really designed to wrap around the wing and rip it off the truck. Skilled drivers can wing the box off the top without touching the first link.

Lastly, and sadly, there is the resigned pessimist who believes there is no hope. We sport battered boxes recovered from the dump, nailed onto an old post that's too short for any good use. We just hope it doesn't get hit with the milk cheque inside.

By the way, what will this winter be like? I saw our snowplough driver down at the hockey game the other day. He was sporting a maniacal grin.

We are in for lots of snow.

Bristlehead

Politics

Political birds inspired by the Canadian national election 2006.

Dear Editor,

I just returned from a walk on the old rail line, and I wanted to send you some thoughts.

It was one of those typical late fall days, slightly overcast and misty, so you can't really see anything clearly and have trouble knowing what's going on.

I was about a kilometre out of town, just made the hill above Frank's corn field when I heard the clatter of geese down the slope. I climbed up the railway embankment and saw a big gaggle of fat old Canada geese. Well, I sat to watch them for a bit. As you know, things are slow in Shelburne, so we need our entertainment where we can get it.

As I sat there watching these birds, it reminded me of Canadian politics. No, I wasn't packing any Creemore lager or some home grown ditch weed or anything; this was just my usual sharp mind at work.

Firstly, the geese were getting fat on someone else's corn. Then they all lumbered into the air and made a big, flashy sweep around the field, jostling for position, and all tried to get next to the leader. This went on until what looked like the second in command whipped them all into line. I noticed they all made noise except the leader. They took off south, as if the USA was all that was on their little minds. Sure seemed like the Liberal Party to me.

All this just began to sink into my mind when I saw a bunch of ducks left behind on the field. Suddenly, they took off as if they just realized the geese had gotten ahead of them. They were the most disorganized bunch you ever wanted to see. The leader flew this way and that, dipping and climbing and floundering. Several others seemed to try to be the leader too.

There was a goose hidden in the bunch, and she suddenly went south after the big gander. All the other ducks quacked in a horrible racket and totally out of synchronization. Sure seemed like the Conservatives to me.

I had barely begun walking further up the line, when a flock of grackles came out of nowhere. Now, here was discipline. They made one solid flock, always moved in unison and produced no sounds that made sense to me. As far as I could tell, they had no visible leader. All seemed uncomfortable, as if they had overstayed their welcome and should have headed home long ago. Sure reminded me of the Bloc Québécois.

I never noticed where they went, back across the river maybe.

Later, a couple of stray sea gulls came over, squawking at each other. Dipping and soaring and wandering around, they seemed to be looking for some direction and maybe the rest of the flock. They made a dive bombing run at me, but fortunately they missed the mark. Unfortunately, their sounds upset me, and they must kept hanging around. Sure reminded me of the Greens.

Well, night threatened, and I headed home. Just as I came through the pines by the ball diamond, a family of night owls spooked from the grass right beside me. They looked like they needed a square meal. This was just typical of these things. You hardly ever see them, and when they make an appearance they scare the hell out of you. I thought of the NDP immediately.

I never did see anything that resembled the Senate, but that place is more like a chicken coop at midnight anyway.

I used to enjoy nature, but the wild just became a whole lot scarier. Now, I'm afraid to go down to the swamp behind George's place. It might remind me of the local council.

If you must vote, think of it as your 12 gauge loaded with bird shot.

Bristlehead

Coyotes

Dear Editor,

It was with some interest I read your news item on November 4th regarding the growing coyote menace here in Dufferin. I can sympathise with local mutton growers who would like "problem" coyotes apprehended dead or alive, well, dead actually. When one's livelihood is threatened, one tends to want effective remedies no matter how extreme.

Dealing with the "problem" coyote problem has a problem. How do you tell a murderous mutton loving coyote from the friendly sweater knitting type? Having once been a hunter of grouse, and only wishing to shoot the "stupid" ones, it was quite a task telling the difference.

"Well Shepherd Jim, what did this problem coyote look like?"

"Well, he was furry with four legs, a tail and an evil grin. He just looked guilty."

I suspect even the most talented professional coyote stalker will have a similar problem. In addition, our wise leaders of the county will have a problem finding a well-qualified talent to embrace the task. Reputedly, the best around is Coyote Pete, but last heard he was working full time in Wiarton shooing black bear away from donut shops. No doubt, we will need to find a similar sharp shooter and avoid the more common gun totter that simply makes ammo manufacturers a good investment.

Apparently, there are three petitions extant regarding this issue. First is the above-mentioned request from the farmer. There is a supporting petition coming from the mice and vole-loving crowd. Their study claims that coyotes spend most of their time eating these adorable little creatures. The last request comes from the well-behaved tea-drinking sweater knitting coyotes who want the county to hire a biologist to identify the bad coyotes and spray them pink, aiding the shooters. Opposition to this comes from a local gin joint that has a popular beverage called the "Pink Coyote". They fear this will leave a bad taste in people's mouths.

The usual political landscape may make it hard to fulfil the farmer's request. The votes may not be there. For instance the mayor of Shelburne will point out there is no "L" in his name and he is not a cruel person. The weatherman in charge of Amaranth is used to putting his finger in the air to check wind direction. Unfortunately, sheep don't make much wind. We will see an interesting debate at council. In the process sheep will die, coyotes will die and political careers may be made and lost. We must remember that although coyotes abhor shepherds, and farmers abhor coyotes, a politician abhors a tough political decision. Perhaps we shouldn't hold our collective breaths on this one.

Bristlehead

Clothes lines

Dear Editor

It has come to my attention that various municipalities or at least sub-division developers have rules against such things as clotheslines. These restrictions upset many; however, I must remind these folks that you cannot fight city hall. The main reason for this is that the favourite expression with most council members is that of my younger grand children: "I didn't do it.", or at best, "The consultant made me do it."

Do not expect support from your neighbours; most of them are concerned with the appearance of Martha Stewart perfection in their little part of suburban nirvana. Remember that even a loose piece of plastic fake wooden façade on someone's house leads to mass meetings and condemnations of builders, trades people and politicians. Apparently the only role for real wood in a new suburban home is a perfectly cut piece of maple, bought from the Esso and to be burnt in the Tiffany fireplace.

There is a perfectly legitimate way around this restriction. The casual observer will have noted mass suburban participation in Canada's national sport, Christmas house decorating, the gaudier the better it appears. Those of us stuck with a pile of wet threads in the Kenmore can take advantage of this annual effort to burn coal in Ohio by running a few strings of lights to the corners of the back yard. Do not worry. Most suburban backyards are the size of an old-fashioned welcome mat so you will have plenty left over. As a concession to your neighbours, some of whom might be named Hatfield or McCoy, be discriminating on what you hang on your strings of seasonal spectacular. For December, I suggest mostly your red frilly items and the wife's boxers with the smiling Santa on them. In my opinion, they will be at least as decorative as eight pieces of birch firewood and branches masquerading as Rudolph.

Once January or April comes around do not fret. A brief look around the neighbourhood shows there are no by-laws as of yet ordering when Christmas decorations must come down, but hurry, this might be included in pending laws controlling vehicle colour by street, forbidding walking to the mail box, smiling at strangers and loud voices such as calling your kids to dinner.

Season's Greetings
Bristlehead

Abhor

Dear Editor,

The English language is a twisted thing as exposed in Doc Brett Reynolds' letter of September 26th. His exploration of abhor was enlightening and humbling, but it strikes me that he missed a few points. For instance, abhor is pronounced somewhat like "a bore" once the H has been scared out of it. There is plenty around Dufferin to scare the H out of things, especially in an election year. As well, abhorred should not be confused with similar sounding phrases such as "I have a bored hole in my head." (This to go along with the normal ones already there, I suppose.). However, lest the condition of my head makes me abhorrent to you, let me quickly change hats. Abhor is the evil twin to adore, something we are all familiar with. For instance, the one who adored us in first year Humber College abhorred us a year later or vice versa if you ended up married.

Doug, your next assignment is to use the word synergy. That should draw Brett out again. Keep it up guys, my television is broken and these are words worth knowing.

Bristlehead

If you have reached this far, thank you.

www.ingramcontent.com/pod-product-compliance
Lightning Source LLC
Chambersburg PA
CBHW071002080526
44587CB00015B/2318